Short Stack Editions | Volume 2

Tomatoes

by Soa Davies

Short Stack Editions

Publisher: Nick Fauchald
Creative Director: Rotem Raffe
Editor: Kaitlyn Goalen
Copy Editor: Abby Tannenbaum
Marketing Manager: Erin Fritch

ISBN: 978-0-9896017-1-9

Printed in Virginia
Fourth printing, July 2017

Table of Contents

From the Editors   5

Introduction   7

Salad
Tomato and Green Olive Tartare   11

Heirloom Tomato Salad with Parmesan Vinaigrette   12

Soup
Green Gazpacho   13

Roasted Tomato Soup   14

Spicy Tomato Consommé   16

Seafood
Grilled Whole Fish with Cherry Tomato Escabeche   18

Baked Lobster Creole   20

Shrimp Ceviche with Tomato Vinaigrette   22

Meat
Baked Tomatoes with Sausage Stuffing   24

Curried Lamb Stew   26

Pan-Roasted Beef Tenderloin with
Caramelized-Tomato Steak Sauce   28

Chinese-Style Pepper Steak   30

Vegetables

Green Tomato Parmesan   32

Tomato and Porcini Ragù with Fresh Pasta   34

Fresh Pasta Dough   35

Preserved

Smoky Tomato Jam   36

Tomato-Anchovy Crostini   36

Oven-Dried Tomatoes   37

Baked Egg with Chorizo & Oven-Dried Tomatoes   37

Canned Tomatoes   38

Basic Tomato Sauce   39

Drink

Wasabi Bloody Marys   40

Dessert

Tomato Tarte Tatin   42

Tomato Sorbet   43

Thank You!   45

Colophon   47

Each summer, photos of immaculate tomatoes dominate the covers of major food magazines. It's easy to get romantic about these heirloom pinups, and even easier to cook with such specimens: As the talented chef Soa Davies says in this edition, the best tomatoes need nothing more than salt, pepper and olive oil.

But we know that this class of pristine, family farm–grown tomatoes is the exception, not the rule. We don't always have time for an heirloom-gathering mission; sometimes the supermarket or corner grocery has to suffice. And our cravings for specific ingredients—especially tomatoes—often don't align with their seasonality.

Short Stack seeks to inspire home cooks by offering delicious, dependable recipes that are in touch with cooking realities. Each volume is filled with techniques, tricks and tips to help you coax the maximum flavor out of an ingredient, whether it be a peak-of-the-season farmers' market find or a year-round pantry staple. Tomatoes happen to be both and, in this edition, Soa has figured out incredibly useful ways to color between those lines.

The tomato-based recipes she created for this volume have already helped us produce meals in our kitchens that outperform the promise of their base materials. We're willing to bet they'll do the same in your kitchen. Happy cooking!

—The Editors

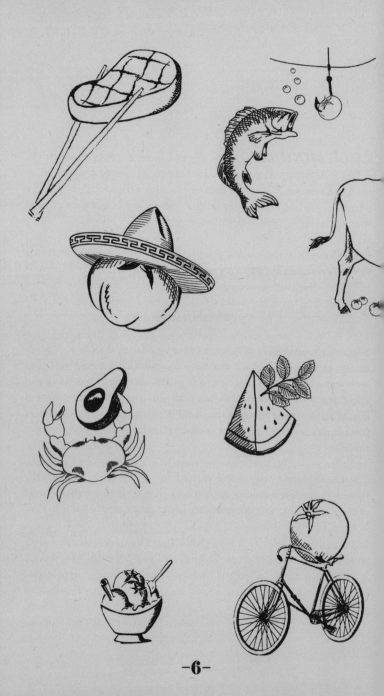

Introduction

I first fell in love with tomatoes when I was a young girl. My mother kept a small garden behind our house, and I would habitually raid her cherry tomato plants, plucking the fruit from the vines and popping them into my mouth. There were other options to choose from—the cherry and apple trees in our garden bore gorgeous fruit—but I looked forward to those first red jewels of summer most of all, and eagerly monitored each plant from the moment it began to flower.

Those first tomatoes made me an addict. They also trapped me as a bit of a purist. To this day, my favorite way to "prepare" tomatoes is by coating them with just salt, pepper and olive oil (and maybe some basil or a curl of Parmesan if I'm feeling ambitious).

It wasn't until I became a chef that I began to appreciate tomatoes' unbelievable versatility in cooking. Each variety has its own unique texture and flavor, and each is best suited to a different preparation. I enjoy using Roma tomatoes for cooking, especially when I'm roasting or baking them. They're firmer and contain less moisture than others, so they maintain their shape better when exposed to high heat. Juicier tomatoes, such as a beefsteak or Brandywine, are great in sauces or salads.

My time in restaurant kitchens redefined my relationship with tomatoes. I suppose the change isn't all that surprising, since tomatoes are rather mysterious, shape-shifting entities. They defy categorization: Scientifically speaking, tomatoes are fruit, but many consider them vegetables—including the United States Supreme Court, which ruled in 1893 that they should be classified as such for customs regulations. They are part of the nightshade family, a motley collection that includes potatoes, chile peppers, eggplants and goji berries. Put simply, tomatoes are a chameleon food, which only adds to their potential in the kitchen.

The recipes in this book represent the spectrum of my love for tomatoes. Some pay tribute to those early cherry tomatoes from my childhood, prepared simply and unadulterated. Others showcase tomatoes as modifier, acting as an agent of flavor in the form of a sauce or edible serving vessel. Many come straight from my home-entertaining repertoire. They are the dishes I turn to when hosting friends and family for a summertime dinner, born out of inspiring hauls from the farmers' market. I hope this book gives you many new ways to enjoy this indispensable ingredient.

—*Soa Davies*

Recipes

Tomato and Green Olive Tartare

I love a good steak tartare, but it's not a dish for everyone. This recipe has all the savory, earthy flavor of the French bistro classic—and it's completely meat-free. Serve the tartare with your favorite cracker or on grilled country bread for a twist on bruschetta.

2 pounds ripe red tomatoes—cored, seeded and finely diced

¾ cup green olives (preferably Picholine), pitted and finely chopped

2 tablespoons chopped capers

1 small shallot, finely minced

½ cup chopped parsley

6 tablespoons extra-virgin olive oil

1 tablespoon sherry vinegar

2 teaspoons Tabasco sauce (optional)

Fine sea salt and freshly ground pepper

Grilled bread or crackers, for serving

serves —4—

In a bowl, combine the tomatoes, olives, capers, shallot, parsley, olive oil, vinegar and Tabasco. Season to taste with salt and pepper.

Using a small ice cream scoop, divide the tartare among four small plates. Alternatively, serve the tartare family-style by placing a large scoop in the center of a plate. Serve with grilled bread or crackers.

Heirloom Tomato Salad with Parmesan Vinaigrette

There are a million tomato salad recipes out there, but this one is my very favorite, both for its simple preparation and the extra-savory complexity the zippy Parmesan vinaigrette adds. The secret to making this salad complete is buying a good variety of tomatoes: I love to mix shapes, sizes and colors of whatever heirlooms are available at the farmers' market.

4 tablespoons red wine vinegar

2 tablespoons fresh lemon juice

1 teaspoon finely minced garlic

½ cup finely grated Parmesan cheese

Fine sea salt and freshly cracked black pepper

6 tablespoons extra-virgin olive oil

2 pounds heirloom tomatoes, assorted sizes and varieties

1 pint cherry tomatoes

¼ cup marjoram leaves, roughly chopped

½ cup flat-leaf parsley leaves

½ cup thinly sliced red onion, soaked in ice water and drained

serves -6-

Place the vinegar, lemon juice and garlic in a mixing bowl and let marinate for 10 minutes, then stir in the Parmesan and 1 tablespoon cracked pepper. Slowly whisk in the olive oil until emulsified. Season to taste with salt. (The vinaigrette can be made up to 3 days ahead and stored in the refrigerator.)

Cut larger tomatoes in half crosswise, then into ¼-inch slices; cut smaller tomatoes into wedges; and cut cherry tomatoes in half. Place the tomatoes in a large bowl and toss with the marjoram, parsley, red onion and vinaigrette. Season to taste with salt and pepper and serve.

Green Gazpacho

This recipe combines two favorites: vitamin-packed green juice and traditional Spanish gazpacho. The bright flavor of green zebra tomatoes balances the sweetness of green grapes to create a refreshing summer soup. I like to serve it with grilled crusty bread or dotted with fresh crab. If you ever go on a juice cleanse, this recipe (minus the garlic) is a restorative way to start the day.

1 pound green zebra tomatoes (6 to 8 small tomatoes)

2 cups chopped romaine lettuce leaves

1 cup green seedless grapes

½ cup flat-leaf parsley leaves

½ cup thinly sliced scallions

¼ cup diced celery

2 tablespoons diced seeded jalapeño (or to taste)

1 teaspoon minced garlic

6 tablespoons sherry vinegar

Fine sea salt and freshly ground black pepper

Extra-virgin olive oil

serves -6-

In a blender or food processor, combine the tomatoes, romaine, grapes, parsley, scallions, celery, jalapeño, garlic and vinegar and puree until smooth. Pass the mixture through a fine-mesh sieve and season to taste with salt and pepper. Refrigerate until chilled.

Divide the gazpacho among six chilled soup bowls, drizzle each with olive oil and serve.

Roasted Tomato Soup

Tomato soup is a panacea that never fails to comfort me. Over the years, I've developed several variations so I can eat it year-round. This roasted tomato soup is fairly traditional, but roasting the tomatoes creates a concentrated flavor that doesn't need much embellishment. For a more refined result, strain the soup through a fine-mesh sieve before you serve it.

5 pounds ripe tomatoes—cored, seeded and chopped

1 large yellow onion, peeled and chopped

1½ cups chopped carrots (about 2 medium)

1½ cups chopped celery (about 3 stalks)

5 cloves garlic, roughly chopped

4 tablespoons extra-virgin olive oil

Fine sea salt and freshly ground black pepper

5 sprigs flat-leaf parsley

4 thyme sprigs

2 bay leaves

1 tablespoon black peppercorns

4 cups chicken stock or vegetable stock

1 cup heavy cream (optional)

serves 8 *to* 10

Preheat the oven to 400°. Combine the tomatoes, onion, carrots, celery and garlic in a large mixing bowl. Drizzle the olive oil over the mixture and season generously with salt and pepper. Toss to coat evenly.

Place the parsley, thyme, bay leaves and peppercorns in the center of a square of cheesecloth; gather the ends and tie with butcher's twine to form a bundle.

Transfer the tomatoes to a roasting pan, add the herb sachet and roast, stirring every 15 minutes, until the vegetables start to caramelize around the edges and are very tender, about 1 to 1½ hours.

Remove the pan from the oven and discard the herb sachet. Stir in the stock, using a spoon to scrape up any pieces of tomato that have caramelized on the bottom of the pan. Working in batches, transfer the mixture to a blender or food processor and puree until smooth. Transfer the soup to a large pot, stir in the cream (if using) and season to taste with salt and pepper. Bring the soup to a simmer and serve hot.

Spicy Tomato Consommé

My tomato consommé is based on tomato water, an amazingly versatile product that can be served hot or cold with a variety of garnishes, depending on your mood.

11 medium tomatoes (about 4 pounds)—cored, seeded and roughly chopped

1 shallot, roughly chopped

2 garlic cloves, roughly chopped

1 jalapeño, seeded and roughly chopped (optional)

½ cup torn basil leaves

1 tablespoon cracked black pepper

Fine sea salt

serves
1

Place the chopped tomatoes in a food processor along with the shallot, garlic, jalapeño, basil and pepper. Pulse until the tomatoes are still chunky but releasing their liquid. Line a fine-mesh sieve with a dampened double layer of cheesecloth and place it over a large container. Pour the chopped tomatoes into the sieve and let drain for 2 to 3 hours, or place in the refrigerator and let drain overnight. Once the liquid has drained, season to taste with salt. Serve hot or cold with the garnishes of your choice.

Some garnish combination suggestions:

Watermelon, mint
and aged balsamic
vinegar (cold)

Chilled crab and
avocado (cold)

Cherry tomatoes, basil and
olive oil (hot or cold)

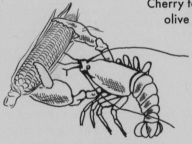

Grilled corn, lobster and
tarragon (hot or cold)

Grilled shrimp,
preserved lemon
and parsley (hot)

Grilled Whole Fish with Cherry Tomato Escabeche

Escabeche may sound foreign and complicated, but it's really just another word for "marinade." This recipe is an adaption of a classic Spanish dish, typically made with sardines, which I love to cook during the summer grilling season. The marinated tomatoes are easy to prepare ahead, so I double the recipe when serving it at large gatherings. If the idea of cooking a whole fish sounds daunting, you can use fish fillets or grilled chicken instead; the escabeche will taste just as good.

½ cup extra-virgin olive oil, divided

1 small yellow onion, thinly sliced

6 garlic cloves, thinly sliced

2 thyme sprigs

1 bay leaf

1 small red Thai chile pepper, halved

Fine sea salt and freshly ground black pepper

½ cup sherry vinegar

2 pints assorted cherry tomatoes, halved lengthwise

Pinch of red pepper flakes

One 3½-to-4-pound whole fish such as snapper or sea bass (ask your fishmonger to scale, gut and remove the gills from the fish)

3 tablespoons canola or vegetable oil, plus more for the grill

1 lemon, halved

serves **4**

In a skillet, warm ¼ cup of the olive oil over medium heat. Add the onion, garlic, thyme, bay leaf and chile and season with salt and pepper. Cook until the onions have softened and browned, about 10 minutes. Stir in the vinegar and the remaining ¼ cup olive oil. Increase the heat and bring to a boil. Add the tomatoes and pepper flakes and simmer for 2 minutes. Remove from the heat and season with salt and pepper. Let the tomatoes sit at room temperature for at least an hour, or refrigerate overnight. Discard the thyme, bay leaf and chile before reheating.

While the tomatoes are marinating, make the fish: Prepare a medium-hot grill and oil the grate. Rub the fish all over with the canola oil and season generously with salt and pepper. Place the fish on the grill and cook until the skin is golden brown, 10 to 12 minutes. Gently turn the fish over and continue grilling until it is cooked through, about 8 to 10 minutes longer. (Check to see if the fish is done by inserting a metal skewer or the tip of a paring knife into the thickest part of the flesh for 5 seconds. If it feels warm to the touch, the fish is ready.) Transfer the fish to a cutting board.

Reheat the tomatoes in a saucepan. Fillet the fish by running a sharp knife lengthwise down its spine, then under the flesh to separate the meat from the bone. Carefully lift off each fillet and place in the center of each dish. Squeeze some lemon juice over each fillet, spoon tomatoes on top and around the fish and serve immediately.

Baked Lobster Creole

I've been lucky enough to spend lots of time in New Orleans, both for fun (too many Jazz Fests to remember) and while producing the food that was featured on the HBO series *Treme*. Here's my take on a Louisiana favorite, shrimp Creole. My version plays up its richness, using lobster in place of shrimp and gilding it with bourbon, another New Orleans staple. Although the recipe requires more preparation and planning than some of the others in this book, it's definitely worth the effort.

Two 2-pound live lobsters

Fine sea salt

½ cup dry white wine

1 tablespoon Creole seasoning

1 head garlic, washed and halved crosswise, plus 1 tablespoon minced garlic

1 onion, peeled and cut in half, plus ½ cup finely diced onion

2 tablespoons canola oil

8 tablespoons (1 stick) butter, divided (2 tablespoons softened)

½ cup finely diced celery (about 1 stalk)

½ cup finely diced red bell pepper

2 tablespoons tomato paste

½ cup bourbon

3 cups peeled and chopped tomatoes

¼ cup Crystal or Tabasco hot sauce

½ teaspoon cayenne pepper

2 teaspoons all-purpose flour

Freshly ground white pepper

serves -4-

Place a lobster on a cutting board. Plunge a chef's knife through the head just above the eyes, then pull the knife downward through the eyes. Twist off the knuckles and claws and reserve. Twist the tail away from the body. Place the tail on the cutting board and split it in half lengthwise. Remove the vein that runs down the center of the tail. Refrigerate the tail until ready to cook, then repeat with the second lobster. Reserve the bodies.

Bring a large stockpot of salted water to a boil. Add the claws and boil for 5 minutes. Transfer the claws to an ice-water bath. When the claws have cooled, separate the knuckles from the claws. Using scissors, cut through the knuckles and remove the meat. Crack the claws and twist to open. Extract the claw meat and reserve along with the knuckle meat.

Place the lobster bodies along with the shells from the claws and knuckles, the white wine, Creole seasoning, garlic halves and onion halves in a saucepan and cover with 5 cups of water. Bring the stock to a boil, then lower the heat and simmer until reduced by half, about 30 minutes. Strain the stock through a fine-mesh sieve, pressing hard on the solids, then discard the solids. You should have 2 cups of stock.

In a saucepan, heat the oil and 2 tablespoons of butter over medium heat. Add the diced onion, celery and bell pepper and cook, stirring, until softened, 5 minutes. Stir in the minced garlic and tomato paste, being careful not to scorch the bottom of the pot. Add the bourbon and simmer until reduced by a little more than half, about 5 minutes. Add the lobster stock, tomatoes, hot sauce and cayenne. Bring the sauce to a boil. Lower the heat and simmer until reduced by half, 30 to 40 minutes. In a bowl, use a fork to blend the 2 tablespoons of softened butter with the flour and slowly stir into the sauce; let the sauce simmer for 5 minutes. Season to taste with salt and pepper.

Preheat the oven to 350°. In a small saucepan, bring ¼ cup of water to a boil. Gradually whisk in the remaining 4 tablespoons of butter, 1 tablespoon at a time, until fully incorporated. Season to taste with salt and pepper. Place the lobster tails in a baking pan, season with salt and pepper and brush with the butter mixture. Bake until the lobster is just opaque, about 5 minutes. Add the lobster claws and knuckles to the saucepan with the remaining butter mixture and keep warm over low heat. Meanwhile, reheat the sauce.

Remover the lobster tails from their shells. Place a piece of lobster tail in the center of each plate and top with knuckle and claw meat. Spoon the sauce over and around the plate and serve immediately.

Shrimp Ceviche with Tomato Vinaigrette

Ceviche is unbeatable on a hot summer day: It's cold, refreshing and requires minimal time in a hot kitchen. This tomato vinaigrette is a great way to dress up shrimp, but it works just as well with other types of fresh seafood. Serve the ceviche with tortilla chips, or, if you want to make a meal of it, spoon it over a half an avocado.

2 pounds small shrimp—peeled, deveined and cut in half lengthwise

Fine sea salt and freshly ground black pepper

1 cup grated tomatoes (from 1 to 2 large tomatoes; see Note)

½ cup fresh lime juice

¼ cup fresh lemon juice

¼ cup fresh orange juice

3 tablespoons sherry vinegar

Pinch of red pepper flakes

½ cup extra-virgin olive oil

¼ cup thinly sliced red onion

1 jalapeño—seeded, stem removed and finely minced

¼ cup chopped cilantro

3 tablespoons thinly sliced chives

serves
-4-

Place the shrimp in a wide, shallow skillet and cover with water. Season heavily with salt and place the pan over medium heat. As soon as the water begins to simmer, transfer the shrimp to a paper-towel-lined container and refrigerate until chilled.

In a medium bowl, stir together the grated tomatoes, lime, lemon and orange juices, vinegar, red pepper flakes and olive oil. Season to taste with salt and pepper and refrigerate. (The tomato vinaigrette can be made a day ahead.)

When the shrimp have cooled completely, transfer them to a large mixing bowl. Add the red onion, jalapeño, cilantro, chives and the tomato vinaigrette and stir to combine. Season to taste with salt and pepper and serve cold.

Note: *To make grated tomatoes: Halve tomatoes crosswise and squeeze out most of the seeds. Using a box grater, coarsely grate the tomatoes into a bowl.*

Baked Tomatoes with Sausage Stuffing

Beefsteak tomatoes might not be as popular or pretty as their heirloom cousins, but their firm flesh and larger size make them ideal for baking. Hollowed out and filled with sausage stuffing, they become the stars of a simple meal. Bonus: Once cooked, the stuffed tomatoes will last up to three days in the refrigerator, and they reheat beautifully.

4 large beefsteak tomatoes

1 cup diced country or sourdough bread

½ cup whole milk

½ pound pork sausage, casing removed

2 tablespoons chopped onion

1 teaspoon chopped garlic

1 egg

4 tablespoons chopped flat-leaf parsley

Fine sea salt and freshly cracked black pepper

2 tablespoons extra-virgin olive oil

½ cup bread crumbs

¼ cup finely grated Parmesan cheese

serves 4

Preheat the oven to 350°. Slice ½ inch off one end of each of the tomatoes, scoop out the pulp and seeds and reserve for another use. (I usually save up the pulp and seeds in a plastic container and freeze for when I'm ready to make a batch of marinara.) Place the tomatoes, cut side up, in a baking dish. Place the diced bread in a bowl and cover with the milk.

Heat a skillet over medium heat and add the sausage. Cook the sausage until well browned, breaking it up with a spatula as it cooks. Add the onion and garlic and continue cooking until the vegetables have softened, about 5 minutes. Let the meat mixture cool slightly, then transfer it to the bowl with the bread and milk. Add the egg, parsley, ¼ teaspoon of salt and two pinches of cracked black pepper. Stir the ingredients to combine.

Drizzle the olive oil over each of the tomatoes and lightly season with salt and pepper. Fill each tomato with some of the sausage mixture and cover the baking dish with foil. Transfer the dish to the oven and bake for 25 minutes.

While the tomatoes are baking, stir the bread crumbs and Parmesan together in a small bowl. After the tomatoes have baked for 25 minutes, top each one with some of the bread-crumb mixture and continue to bake for another 10 to 15 minutes or until the topping is golden brown and toasted. Transfer to plates and serve.

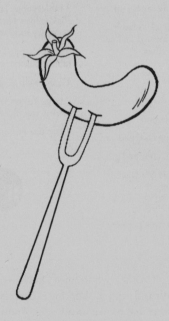

Curried Lamb Stew

I have a confession to make: I used to hate curry. I spent years dodging invitations to Indian restaurants just so I wouldn't have to admit my shameful secret. But during my years at Le Bernardin, I slowly learned to appreciate curry and its many variations, especially the Caribbean-style curries that are finished with coconut milk. The recipe here reminds me of one of my favorite street carts in New York, the Jamaican Dutchy, which serves a fantastic goat curry.

4 tablespoons canola oil

3 pounds boneless lamb shoulder, trimmed and cut into 1-inch cubes

Fine sea salt and freshly ground black pepper

1 cup diced carrots

1 cup diced onion

2 tablespoons chopped garlic

1 tablespoon chopped ginger

3 tablespoons Madras curry powder

½ teaspoon allspice

Pinch of cayenne pepper

3 tablespoons Jamaican Pickapeppa sauce (available in specialty food stores or online)

5 cups chopped tomatoes (about 6 large tomatoes)

1½ cups chicken stock

2 large Yukon Gold potatoes, peeled and diced (about 2 cups)

1 cup unsweetened coconut milk

serves 6 to 8

Heat the canola oil in a heavy-bottomed Dutch oven or stockpot. Season the lamb with salt and pepper. Working in batches, add the lamb to the pot in a single layer and brown on all sides. Transfer to a plate and set aside.

Add the carrots and onion to the pot and cook over medium heat until tender and just starting to brown, about 5 to 7 minutes. Add the garlic and ginger and cook until fragrant, 2 to 3 minutes. Add the curry powder, allspice and cayenne and cook, stirring, until fragrant, about 1 minute. Add the browned lamb and cover with the Pickapeppa sauce, chopped tomatoes and chicken stock. Bring the stew to a simmer and cook for 45 minutes, then add the potatoes and coconut milk and simmer until the lamb and potatoes are tender, about 15 to 25 minutes longer. Divide the stew among bowls and serve.

Pan-Roasted Beef Tenderloin with Caramelized-Tomato Steak Sauce

I am not a big meat eater, but there are times when nothing less than a juicy steak will satisfy me. This is my recipe for those moments. By caramelizing the tomatoes and dousing them in Worcestershire, they act as both a vegetable and steak sauce, beating out anything that comes in a bottle by a long shot.

Four 6-ounce filets mignon

Fine sea salt and freshly ground black pepper

Herbes de Provence

2 large beefsteak tomatoes

1 teaspoon sugar

3 tablespoons extra-virgin olive oil

3 tablespoons Worcestershire sauce

1 small shallot, finely minced

1 tablespoon finely chopped garlic

2 tablespoons unsalted butter

3 tablespoons red wine vinegar

serves
-4-

Preheat the oven to 400°. Generously season the steaks on all sides with salt, pepper and herbes de Provence and let the steaks come to room temperature, about 15 to 20 minutes.

Core the tomatoes, trim off the top and bottom of each and cut them in half crosswise. Season the tomato halves with salt, pepper and sugar. Heat the olive oil in an heavy-bottomed ovenproof skillet until very hot. Remove the pan from the heat and carefully add the seasoned tomatoes to the pan, cut-side down. Place the skillet in the oven and roast the tomatoes until caramelized and cooked through, about 15 to 20 minutes. Halfway through cooking, turn the tomatoes over and spoon the Worcestershire sauce over them.

Heat a cast-iron skillet over very high heat until almost smoking. Add the steaks to the pan and sear on all sides until deeply browned, then place the skillet in the oven and continue cooking until an instant-read thermometer inserted in the meat reaches 120° to 125° for medium rare, about 7 to 8 minutes. Transfer the steaks to a cutting board and let rest for at least 5 minutes.

While the steaks rest, add the shallot, garlic and butter to the skillet the steaks were cooked in. Cook over medium heat, stirring, until the shallot has softened, about 1 minute. Deglaze the pan with the vinegar, then add the caramelized tomatoes along with their juices. Bring the sauce to a boil, turn off the heat and season to taste with salt and pepper.

Divide the steaks among plates and top each with a caramelized tomato. Spoon the remaining sauce over and around each steak and serve.

Chinese-Style Pepper Steak

This is one of my favorite recipes to cook when I'm in a hurry to get dinner on the table. It takes about the same amount of time to pull together as ordering takeout from my local Chinese restaurant, and the result is so much better. Tomatoes play an essential role in the recipe, as they mix with the soy sauce to make a beautiful sauce for this fast, healthy and delicious dish.

4 tablespoons soy sauce

2 tablespoons oyster sauce (optional)

3 tablespoons rice wine vinegar

1 tablespoon cornstarch

Pinch red pepper flakes

Fine sea salt and freshly cracked black pepper

2 tablespoons canola oil

1 green bell pepper, thinly sliced

1 red bell pepper, thinly sliced

1 small yellow onion, halved and thinly sliced

2 cloves garlic, peeled and thinly sliced

8 ounces sirloin or flank steak, cut into ⅛-inch slices

1 cup diced Roma tomatoes

¼ cup fresh basil leaves, torn

Cooked white rice, for serving

serves
-4-

In a small bowl, stir together the soy sauce, oyster sauce (if using), vinegar, cornstarch, red pepper flakes and ½ teaspoon black pepper.

Heat the canola oil in a wok or cast-iron skillet over high heat. Add the peppers, onion and garlic and stir-fry for 1 minute. Add the beef and stir-fry for 1 minute, then add the tomatoes and cook for 1 minute longer. Add the soy-sauce mixture and toss to combine. Sprinkle with the basil and season to taste with salt. Serve immediately with rice.

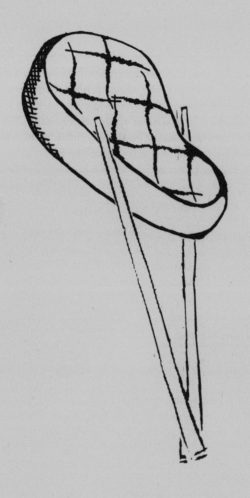

Green Tomato Parmesan

For most people, green (or under-ripened) tomatoes begin and end with a dip in the fryer. This recipe pushes them even further: Since the moisture content of a green tomato is similar to that of eggplant, I use them in a twist on eggplant Parmesan. The combination of the tomatoes' tangy flavor, the rich tomato sauce and the mozzarella makes for a great vegetarian meal.

serves **6**

2½ to 3 pounds green tomatoes, cut crosswise into ½-inch-thick slices

Fine sea salt and freshly ground black pepper

1 cup fine bread crumbs

1 cup freshly grated Parmesan, divided

½ teaspoon dried oregano

Pinch of cayenne pepper

½ cup all-purpose flour

2 eggs, beaten

6 tablespoons extra-virgin olive oil

3 tablespoons canola oil

2½ cups Basic Tomato Sauce (see page 39)

1 cup basil leaves

1 cup shredded mozzarella

Preheat the oven to 375°. Season the tomato slices with salt and pepper.

In a bowl, stir together the bread crumbs, ½ cup of the Parmesan, the oregano and cayenne. Season with salt and pepper. Place the bread-crumb mixture, flour and eggs into three separate shallow pans. Dredge the tomatoes in flour, then dip them in the egg to thoroughly coat, letting the excess drip off. Dredge the tomatoes in the bread crumbs and shake off any excess.

In a large nonstick skillet, heat the olive and canola oils over medium heat until shimmering. Working in batches, add the tomatoes in a single layer and fry until they're golden brown, about 2 minutes; flip the tomatoes and fry them an additional 2 minutes or until both sides are golden brown. Transfer the tomatoes to a paper-towel-lined plate.

Line the bottom of a 9-by-13-inch baking dish with ½ cup of tomato sauce and top with a single layer of fried tomatoes. Scatter half of the basil leaves on top. Spread about 1 cup of tomato sauce over the tomatoes and basil. Sprinkle the remaining ½ cup of the Parmesan and ½ cup of the mozzarella on top of the sauce. Repeat with the rest of the tomatoes to make another layer and top with the remaining sauce, basil and mozzarella.

Transfer the dish to the oven and bake until the sauce is bubbling around the edges and the cheese starts to brown, about 15 to 20 minutes. Let the Green Tomato Parmesan sit for at least 5 minutes before cutting into slices and serving.

Tomato and Porcini Ragù with Fresh Pasta

I have a love-hate relationship with pasta: I love the taste but hate the way it makes my body feel (I'm gluten-intolerant). Fortunately, I have no such ambivalence about pasta sauce. This ragù is rich with pancetta and earthy porcini mushrooms but elegant in its simplicity. If you have a hard time finding porcini mushrooms, use another variety (such as cremini) and add an ounce of rehydrated dried porcinis. The homemade pasta is just a bonus, so feel free to use high-quality store-bought pasta.

3 tablespoons extra-virgin olive oil

½ cup diced pancetta

1 medium onion, diced

¼ cup thinly sliced garlic cloves

1 pound fresh porcini mushrooms (or mushroom of your choice), diced

2 bay leaves

½ cup dry red wine

2 cups chopped fresh tomatoes or canned diced tomatoes

2 tablespoons chopped flat-leaf parsley

1 pound fresh pasta (recipe follows)

Parmesan cheese, for grating

serves 6

Heat the oil in a large heavy saucepan or Dutch oven over high heat. Add the pancetta and cook until golden brown. Add the onion, garlic, mushrooms and bay leaves and continue to cook, stirring frequently, until the onion is lightly browned. Add the red wine and simmer until the mixture is almost dry. Stir in the tomatoes and parsley, reduce the heat to low and simmer very gently, stirring occasionally, until the sauce has thickened, 45 minutes to 1 hour. Season to taste with salt and pepper.

Cook the pasta in a large pot of boiling salted water until al dente, about 2 minutes. Drain the pasta and transfer it to the pan with the sauce and gently toss to coat. Serve with freshly grated Parmesan cheese.

Fresh Pasta Dough

2 cups all-purpose flour, plus more for dusting

6 large egg yolks

Pinch of fine sea salt

makes
1
pound

Make a mound of flour in the center of a clean work surface. Make a well in the center of the mound and add the yolks to the well. Stir in the salt and, using a fork, slowly work in the flour from the edges until it is fully incorporated and a dough forms. Knead the dough, adding more flour as necessary, until silky and smooth. (Alternatively, all of the ingredients can be put into a food processor fitted with a dough blade and pulsed until the dough forms.) Pat the dough into a flat rectangle, wrap tightly in plastic wrap and refrigerate for at least 20 minutes.

Using a rolling pin, flatten and shape the dough into a ¼-inch-thick rectangle. Using a manual pasta machine set on the widest setting, slowly crank the handle while feeding the dough through the rollers. Gently guide the dough as it comes out. Fold the dough in half and repeat this process 4 to 5 times or until the dough is very smooth and silky.

When the dough feels very soft to the touch, cut it in half and cover one half with a damp towel. Roll the other half of dough through the pasta machine, progressively adjusting the rollers to thinner widths, one setting at a time, until the sheet of pasta is slightly thicker than paper. Cut the pasta into 12-inch-long sheets and stack them, dusting each sheet with flour to prevent sticking. Repeat the process with the remaining dough.

Cut the sheets of pasta into the desired width.

Note: The pasta can be made up to a week ahead and frozen on a tray with a generous dusting of flour and tightly wrapped in plastic. The frozen pasta can go directly into the boiling water.

Preserving Tomatoes

When the late-summer tomato bounty arrives, I like to put some away for those months when my fresh tomato options are pink and taste like cardboard. Here are a couple of ways to make the flavor of summer last.

Smoky Tomato Jam

This is an easy but unique condiment that can be used on virtually anything. I like to serve it with cheese (especially goat cheese), in place of ketchup on burgers or on a BLT for a classic with a kick.

6 cups peeled, seeded and diced tomatoes (about 8 large tomatoes)

¾ cup sugar

½ cup sherry vinegar

3 tablespoons smoked salt

2 tablespoons smoked paprika

makes 3 cups

Place all of the ingredients in a heavy-bottomed stainless steel pot and simmer over low heat, stirring occasionally, until thickened and almost dry, about 1 hour. Transfer to an airtight container and refrigerate for up to 2 weeks.

Tomato-Anchovy Crostini

8 slices crusty bread, sliced ½-inch thick

Extra-virgin olive oil

8 tablespoons Smoky Tomato Jam

16 vinegar-cured white anchovy fillets (*boquerones*)

Fresh flat-leaf parsley leaves, for garnish

serves 4

Preheat the oven to 350°. Place the bread slices on a baking sheet and drizzle with olive oil. Transfer to the oven and lightly toast, about 3 to 5 minutes. On each slice of bread, spread a tablespoon of the Smoky Tomato Jam and top with two anchovy fillets. Garnish with the parsley and serve.

Oven-Dried Tomatoes

20 Roma tomatoes

5 garlic cloves, thinly sliced

6 to 8 thyme sprigs

Fine sea salt and freshly ground black pepper

Extra-virgin olive oil

Preheat the oven to 275° and line a rimmed baking sheet with parchment paper. Bring a large pot of water to a boil. Using a paring knife, cut a shallow X on the bottom of each tomato. Add the tomatoes to the pot and blanch for about 20 seconds, then transfer to an ice-water bath. When the tomatoes have cooled, peel, core them and squeeze out the seeds, then cut the tomatoes in half crosswise.

Place the tomatoes in a large mixing bowl along with the garlic and thyme. Season to taste with salt and pepper and drizzle enough olive oil over the tomatoes to generously coat them. Place the tomatoes in a single layer on the prepared baking sheet and bake for 2 to 2½ hours, until they're lightly caramelized and a bit dry to the touch. Let the tomatoes cool completely, then transfer them to Mason jars or airtight containers and cover completely with olive oil.

Baked Egg with Chorizo & Oven-Dried Tomatoes

serves
-1-

3 oven-dried tomato halves, coarsely chopped

Chopped chives (optional)

1 egg

Fine sea salt and freshly ground black pepper

2 thin slices Spanish chorizo (substitute prosciutto if necessary)

Preheat the oven to 350°. Mix the tomatoes with the chives in a small ramekin. Crack the egg over the tomatoes and season with salt and pepper; top with the chorizo and bake until the egg is just barely set, about 10 to 15 minutes. Serve immediately.

Canning Your Own Tomatoes

I will always say that fresh produce is better than preserved. But in the dead of winter, when your only fresh tomato option is those anemic-looking pink orbs at the supermarket, it's better to go with canned tomatoes for soups and sauces. San Marzano tomatoes tend to have the biggest flavor of all the canned options (just make sure the can has the words "Pomodoro San Marzano dell'Agro Sarnese Nocerino D.O.P" on it). Better still, buy a crate of tomatoes in the peak of their summer season and can them at home to use year-round in dishes like my Basic Tomato Sauce.

Canned Tomatoes

20 pounds ripe tomatoes

½ cup fresh lemon juice

Special Equipment:

5 to 6 quart-size canning jars with lids, sterilized

Stockpot or pressure canner

Bring a large stockpot full of water to a boil. Cut a shallow X on the bottom of each tomato. Add the tomatoes to the pot and blanch for about 20 seconds, then transfer to a bowl of ice water. Peel the tomatoes.

Separate one quarter of the tomatoes and, working in batches, puree in a food processor. Strain the juice, discarding the pulp and seeds, and reserve the juice (you should have about 1 quart of juice).

Fill the jars with peeled tomatoes, leaving about ½ inch of room below the lip of the jar.

Divide the lemon and tomato juices evenly among the jars. If necessary, top with water to barely cover the tomatoes.

Tap the jars to remove any air bubbles. Seal the jars (but not too tightly), place them in a very large stockpot and cover with water. Bring the water to a boil and cook, adding water as necessary to keep the jars covered, for 45 minutes. If you're using a pressure canner, cook according to the manufacturer's directions, depending on the amount of pressure used. Tomatoes will last up to two weeks in the refrigerator, or longer if made using the pressure-canning method.

Basic Tomato Sauce

¼ cup extra-virgin olive oil

5 garlic cloves, finely chopped

2 shallots, finely chopped

6 cups Roma (or canned) tomatoes—peeled, seeded and diced

1 teaspoon dried oregano, crumbled

1 teaspoon sugar

2 tablespoons red wine vinegar

Fine sea salt and freshly ground black pepper

makes
6
quarts

In a medium saucepan, heat the olive oil. Add the garlic and shallots and cook over medium-low heat until softened, about 4 minutes. Add the tomatoes, oregano, sugar and vinegar. Bring the mixture to a boil, then remove from the heat and season to taste with salt and pepper.

This is a great sauce for pizza or pasta.

Wasabi Bloody Marys

Some of these ingredients might be unfamiliar, but it's entirely worth seeking them out to make this bracing, Japanese-influenced take on brunch's most popular cocktail. If you can't find the yuzu juice or yuzu kosho (a Japanese condiment made with yuzu and chile peppers), don't worry: Just add another dash of Tabasco. But don't improvise with the wasabi: It's important to use fresh or prepared wasabi instead of the powder, since the latter will change the consistency of the mix. Cheers!

1½ cups fresh tomato juice (*see Note*)

2 tablespoons wasabi paste

1 teaspoon yuzu kosho (available from most Asian markets or online)

½ cup yuzu juice or lemon juice

3 tablespoons soy sauce

3 tablespoons Tabasco sauce

Salt and freshly ground black pepper

10 ounces vodka

Japanese pickles, for garnish

makes 4 cocktails

In a large pitcher, whisk together the tomato juice, wasabi paste, yuzu kosho, yuzu juice, soy sauce and Tabasco sauce. Season to taste with salt and pepper.

Fill four tall glasses with ice. In a cocktail shaker filled with ice, combine 2½ ounces of vodka with 4 ounces of the Bloody Mary mix and shake gently. Strain into one of the glasses, then repeat to make three more cocktails. Garnish each glass with a spear of Japanese pickle and serve.

Note: To make fresh tomato juice, place 2 to 3 medium tomatoes in a blender and puree until smooth. Strain through a fine-mesh sieve, pressing on the solids, and reserve the juice.

Tomato Tarte Tatin

It's easy to forget that tomatoes are actually fruit and, as such, can (and should!) be eaten for dessert. One of my favorite desserts of all time is tarte Tatin. Butter, caramel, puff pastry: What's not to love? This recipe uses firm Roma tomatoes in place of the usual apples. The addition of the balsamic vinegar gives the slightly savory tomatoes a wonderful kick, and the tomato sorbet adds freshness. Vanilla ice cream will also work beautifully if you're not feeling up to making the sorbet.

10 Roma tomatoes

6 tablespoons unsalted butter

¾ cup sugar

2 tablespoons balsamic vinegar

1 sheet puff pastry dough,
cut into an 8-inch disk

Preheat the oven to 400°. Bring a large pot of water to a boil. Using a paring knife, cut a shallow X on the bottom of each tomato. Add the tomatoes to the pot and blanch for about 20 seconds, then transfer to an ice-water bath. When the tomatoes have cooled, peel and slice each in half lengthwise.

In a heavy-bottomed 8-inch skillet (preferably cast-iron), heat the butter over medium-high heat until it starts to turn brown and smell nutty. Sprinkle the sugar evenly over the pan and cook until it turns golden brown, about 5 to 10 minutes. Stir in the vinegar. Place the tomato halves, cut side up, in a circular pattern in the caramel and continue cooking until the tomatoes have softened, about 5 minutes.

Turn off the heat and top the tomatoes with the disk of puff pastry. Bake the tart until the pastry is a deep golden brown, about 20 to 25 minutes. Let the tart rest for at least 5 minutes in the pan. Place a large plate or platter over the tarte and quickly but carefully flip it onto the plate.

Serve warm with vanilla ice cream or Tomato Sorbet (recipe follows).

Tomato Sorbet

1 cup sugar

¼ cup light corn syrup

2 cups fresh tomato juice (see Note)

¼ cup fresh lemon juice

Salt

In a saucepan, bring ½ cup of water to a boil, remove from the heat and stir in the sugar and corn syrup until the sugar has completely dissolved. Let cool completely.

In a bowl, stir together the syrup, tomato juice, lemon juice and a pinch of salt. Freeze the sorbet in an ice cream maker according to manufacturer's directions.

Note: To make fresh tomato juice, place 3 to 4 medium tomatoes in a blender and puree until smooth. Strain through a fine-mesh sieve, pressing on the solids, and reserve the juice.

Thank You!

Short Stack gives its endless gratitude to those who inspired us to create a new kind of food publication, and its deepest thanks to those who helped us see it through: Julia and Paul Child, Ashley Christensen, Charman Driver, William Hereford, Jordan McIntyre, Mom, Alyssa Pagano, Bonnie Slotnick, Abby Tannenbaum, Frank Thompson, Tina Ujlaki, Will Schwalbe and the folks at the YAI Network.

The author would like to thank Celeste Brown, Carmindy, Tracy Cowardin, Sarah Devito, Mark Meyer, Annette Seagraves and Jina Yurgosky "for being my guinea pigs and always supporting me."

You wouldn't be holding this book without the generosity and enthusiasm of our 1,761 Kickstarter backers, including those who gave a little extra to be named here: Scott Hocker, Victoria Hunton, Juliana Minium, Kitty Morgan, Shannen Naegel, Robert Rembert, Carrie Ross, Heidi Swanson, Brandy Valdez and Cliff Wu.

Share your Short Stack cooking experiences with us
(or just keep in touch) via:

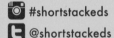

#shortstackeds   facebook.com/shortstackeditions

@shortstackeds   hello@shortstackeditions.com

Colophon

This edition of Short Stack was printed by Stephen Gould Corp. in Richmond, Virginia on Mohawk Britehue Ultra Lava (interior) and Neenah Oxford White (cover) paper. The main text of the book is set in Futura and Jensen Pro, and the headlines are set in Lobster.

Available now at ShortStackEditions.com:

Vol. 1 | Eggs,
by Ian Knauer

Vol. 2 | Tomatoes,
by Soa Davies

Vol. 3 | Strawberries,
by Susan Spungen

Vol. 4 | Buttermilk,
by Angie Mosier

Vol. 5 | Grits,
by Virginia Willis

Vol. 6 | Sweet Potatoes,
by Scott Hocker

Vol. 7 | Broccoli,
by Tyler Kord

Vol. 8 | Honey,
by Rebekah Peppler

Vol. 9 | Plums,
by Martha Holmberg

Vol. 10 | Corn,
by Jessica Battilana

Vol. 11 | Apples,
by Andrea Albin

Vol. 12 | Brown Sugar,
by Libbie Summers

Vol. 13 | Lemons,
by Alison Roman

Vol. 14 | Prosciutto di Parma,
by Sara Jenkins

Vol. 15 | Summer Squash,
by Sarah Baird

Vol. 16 | Peaches,
by Beth Lipton

Vol. 17 | Chickpeas,
by Victoria Granof

Vol. 18 | Chocolate,
by Susie Heller

Vol. 19 | Maple Syrup,
by Casey Elsass

Vol. 20 | Rhubarb,
by Sheri Castle

Vol. 21 | Cherries,
by Stacy Adimando

Vol. 22 | Eggplant,
by Raquel Pelzel

Vol. 23 | Tahini,
by Adeena Sussman

Vol. 24 | Ginger,
by Mindy Fox

Vol. 25 | Avocados,
by Katie Quinn

Vol. 26 | Peanuts,
by Steven Satterfield

Vol. 27 | Coconut,
by Ben Mims

Vol. 28 | Cucumbers,
by Dawn Perry

Vol. 29 | Pears,
by Andrea Slonecker